BEHIND THE SMILE

A Collection of Poems

BEHIND THE SMILE

A Collection of Poems

— SHANTA DUTTA ROY —

EMBASSY BOOKS
www.embassybooks.in

Behind the Smile © Shanta Dutta Roy

First Edition 2019

Published in India by:
Embassy Book Distributors
120, Great Western Building,
Maharashtra Chamber of Commerce Lane,
Fort, Mumbai 400 023, India
Tel: (+9122) -30967415, 22819546
Email: info@embassybooks.in
www.embassybooks.in

ISBN: 978-93-88247-48-1

All rights reserved. No part of this publication may be
reproduced, distributed, or transmitted in any form or by any
means, including photocopying, recording, or other electronic or
mechanical methods, without the prior written permission of the
publisher. The use of brief quotations embodied in reviews
is permitted.

Cover Design by Sonal Churi

Layout and typesetting by Sonal Churi & Gangaram Dhuri

Illustrations by Sunil Pujari and Paresh Churi

Printed & Bound in India by Repro India Ltd., Navi Mumbai

Acknowledgements

It is with a great deal of pleasure that I put on record my thanks to all those who wanted to see the poems in print, especially my family and friends whose response in many forms has enriched me greatly.

My special gratitude goes out to you Mr. Joe for your tremendous support and patience. Despite your own work pressures and responsibilities, you organised everything to a T. Thank you so very much.

Thanks Mr. Mahendra Belekar and Ms. Reena Varghese for helping me out with your deft computer skills.

My special thanks to Mr. Sohin Lakhani for agreeing to publish the book.

And thank you Bikash, my mainstay.

Foreword

Wordsworth said " Poetry is the spontaneous overflow of powerful feelings." I believe, it is very true of my poetry. Times are changing rapidly. The tranquil times of our childhood are fast giving way to tumultuous times. One feels anger, exasperation, angst at times and yet at others, there is a deep feeling of gratification at the fighting spirit displayed by ordinary men and women. A restless mind mulls over all the myriad events happening all around. The outpouring of emotions is natural. A sensitive soul pours out his or her feelings through painting, music or the power of the pen. And my feelings take the form of poetry. When I shared some of these poems with my family members and friends, some of them, in spite of not having a background in literature, read them with keen interest and waited for some more. Who says poetry is not popular?

So, with the hope that readers will find the poems readable, I dedicate the collection to them.

— **Shanta Dutta Roy**

Contents

1. A decision   11
2. No place in the Sun   13
3. Not anymore   18
4. I am no Sita   20
5. End of a quest   23
6. At the crossing   27
7. Faith   31
8. Unpaid dues   34
9. Love abandoned   36
10. Them and me   39
11. Narrow strip of sky   44
12. Dreams cheat   49
13. The confluence   52
14. Childhood reclaimed   54
15. The burning hall   55
16. The vacant space   59
17. My father   61
18. Parallel lines   65
19. My shame   67
20. A truth   69
21. The rising and setting sun   71
22. My Valentine's Day   75
23. Embrace life   81

Contents

24. Sign of our times   83

25. Birth of a song   85

26. Born a woman   86

27. Billoo   88

28. The last afternoon   91

29. The theft   94

30. The leaf-hopper   96

31. Autumnal leaves   97

32. The flag   99

33. Then and now   103

34. Lying buried   106

35. Lesson learnt   107

36. The morning after   109

37. The pebbles   111

38. The dawn must come   112

39. Identity   115

40. I know why   117

41. That's me   120

42. Hope   122

43. Oxygen for life   125

44. A kaleidoscope   127

45. A job to do   129

A decision

You tried to placate your child —
sullen, pouting, holding on to the
corner of your sari
with promises of goodies
in the evening.
The super-man figure
both of you saw in the Kids Zone
in the Mall the other day;
and the yellow police car
blowing the siren as it raced past;
followed by the ice-cream cone
of strawberry flavour,
one of his favourites.

Today specially you need to reach early
presentations and meetings are
lined up for the day—
bouquets to be picked up on the way
for the visiting Director, a bachelor himself
hardly the kind to empathise

with a working mother multi-tasking
—leaving behind a part of her every morning
torn between two sets of moral forces—
a toddler left in the care of a help
and making a success of a job
as demanding as hers.

As she negotiates the traffic on the way,
her grip on the steering hardens.
She will not feel sorry for herself.
Will not let her conscience prick her daily
as it doesn't her husband.
She will stop being on a guilt-trip endlessly.
And this time she manoeuvres
the turn effortlessly.

No place in the Sun

She has brought it
upon herself,
choosing to dress up
the way she did,
wearing torn jeans and a top
and sometimes a mini skirt.

She is the glow worm
tempting the oh, such gullible boys.
Her kohl-lined eyes,
the arched eye-brows
and luscious lips—
the buxom bomb-shell
that she is—
is sure-shot recipe
for disaster.

Protect your sons, mothers
put the evil-warding kajal dot,
ensure they come back to you
before sunset.

The siren is out there
to entice them
with her wily charm
promising the forbidden fruit.

Why did they not let me be mother?
Why do I have to carry the cross
for wanting my place in the sun?
It was my choice not to be
ashamed of my body.
Not to cover myself up in the
six-yard sari—
but dress up in something
that is functional and smart
on the contrary.
Is this why the coward,
the bully disfigured me, mama?
Is it because he didn't know
how to handle me?
Not sure how his mom
would react

to a daughter-in-law
who might not stay
within the permissible limits?
Is it why the darling mama's boy
decided to scar such girls
for life—girls they want
to take to bed,
but cower to marry?
Saving all his brotherhood
from such women with that
one stroke?

I cried out mother
seeing myself in the mirror,
hideous to sight and touch
that children get scared of
and men revolted.

Want you to cuddle your princess
once more mama as you used to—
everytime she was bullied in school;
telling her the world would change.

Want to grow wings
one more time mother
and fly, but this time
higher and higher
till I can hug the star
that is shining the brightest
in the sky.

Not anymore

Too much grief can dry up your tears
they say.
The natives of Iraq,
Syria or Afghanistan,
or our very own Kashmir
will never know again
what tears are.
Inhabitants of ghost-cities
with iconic monuments razed;
eyes of hapless frightened children
large with unshed tears.
They have seen only bomb-blasts
and suicide-attacks;
their near-and-dear ones
lost in mindless frenzy;
cheap blood flowing on the bazaar streets
mingling with the waters of Euphrates,
Tigris or Amu Darya,
the serene Jhelum or Chenab rivers.

Their tears don't roll,
hearts don't break anymore
as they are frozen in time and space.

No.
Their capacity for suffering
is not saturated yet.
They have not yet become
stone-numb.
I have seen them cry
in the silence of the grave-yard
and the eternal resting place of the Hindus
while lighting a candle or
placing a flower,
praying and hoping
the marauders and murderers
will see light of reason again;
the seasonal flowers will blossom
in the gardens of Babylon,
the Babur park in Kabul
the Shalimar and Chinar gardens
in Kashmir.

The soil will be moisturised
by the waters of the rivers again
not by the blood of the masses
Anymore.

I am no Sita

How I wish to travel back in time
when a prince could gladly
walk the path of thorns
to honour a father's word.
When one brother could choose
to spend fourteen years
in deprivation
to guard and protect him.
And another renounce the throne
that was not
rightfully his own.

How I wish to travel back in time
when a son's sense of filial duty
could make him carry
his blind infirm parents
to places of pilgrimage.
While the story of a young boy's
thirst for knowledge,
making him gladly cut off his thumb
can only make one numb.

But I know I can't —
carry as I must
the cross of my previous birth—
wash as I have to
the sins of my past.
So I'm made to see everyday
parents sacrificed
at the altar of children's
ambition and apathy.
Brother killing brother
violence and holocaust
putting to shame
the cruelty of a
marauding Nadirshah
or an Aurangzeb.

Little girls, hardly out
of their nursery
raped and butchered
by depraved perverts.
Little boys, equally vulnerable

once out of the safety
of their homes.

How many deaths I have died
witnessing the moral turpitude
of a generation
that boasts of advancement.
How many times I have wished
the earth would open up
and swallow me in.

But that, I know
will not happen
as it happens
only in our Puranas
and I am no Sita
of our Ramayana.

End of a quest

A vast congregation
sitting cross-legged on the floor
singing bhajans as if in a frenzy.
Some playing the tabla,
some harmonium and others the khanjar.
If someone like me wants to find peace
in God's abode
Then this surely is not the place.

Passing by a gurdwara
the sound of shabad Kirtan
over the microphone
fills me with the same desire
to go some place else.

Nestled as my housing block is
between a mosque and a church
I sit up with a start often
when the mullahs call the devouts
to the mosque
in an unearthly hour in the morn.

When the Sunday masses
are conducted five times a day
again over the mike
the same question comes to my mind.
does God not like the peaceful prayers
of His devotees?
True.
The places are all sanctified
and hundreds throng there everyday.
Surely they get what they seek.

Am I the unholy one
—the agnostic
trivialising the piety
of the people?

Surely not.
But what about my struggles?
My conflicts?
I too had set out
to search for my God,
seeking their resolution.

I have failed to find Him
in all this noise and din.

Now I seek and cling
to my God
in parks and play-fields
among children and urchins
in the lanes and by-lanes
of our cities and towns.

At the crossing

I see them everyday
waving the day's newspaper
or 'India Today',
as I stop at the traffic intersection
for the light to change.

On other days
it is a bouquet of
somewhat wilted red roses
wrapped in cellophane
that they try to sell.

But touch us they can't,
—not physically;
ensconced as we are
in the cocoon of our cars
safely.

Their dirty hands
cannot sully
our scented, near-perfect
world.

Neither can they fill our nostrils
with their suffocatingly
nauseating smell.
But emotionally?
Don't they touch us
emotionally?
Don't they touch a raw nerve
somewhere?
They do, you bet.
The vacant look
in the eyes of the emaciated baby
in her mother's arms,
too hungry and exhausted
to let out even a wailing cry.

The image of the barefoot girl
with unkempt hair
and shabby clothes;
the slightly older boy
her brother may be—
selling dark car-window screens

haunt me on many a night
as I toss and turn in bed
wondering if they too
don't have dreams.

Dreams to march
with the rest of the nation
to a bright and glorious
tomorrow—

If only Fate had willed it so.
Or perhaps if you and I
joined hands together
to make them equal partners
in the success story
that is India today.

Faith

The wailing siren of the ambulance
sounds a note of urgency;
quitening the noisy vibrant market place,
drivers hurriedly clear the way
as if in awe.

Who is in there—
under the white sheet
with oxygen mask
and saline drips?
'Will he make it?'
The question is writ large
on the faces of passers-by.

In the sanitised, sterilised
white corridors of hospital
the staff in white,
pushing the trolley
straight to the operation theatre,
past the gigantic meter box
with a skull-and-bones image

stimulates further
the curiosity
of patient's many relatives
'Will he make it?'

The sign on the door of the
OT too is ominous.
A stern "No Entry"—
typical of a hospital—
brief, succinct, precise.

With plucky patience
she waits
with stony gaze.
Nothing can intimidate her.
Neither the eerie stillness of the place
nor the whispers of the staff
in crisp, white dress
nor even the ominous signs
all around.

If there is God on earth
It is he—the Doctor.
He may not be the creator
but is the only one
who can give
your precious one
another chance to live.

Unpaid dues

That your blood is flowing
through my veins, my arteries
I'm proud of that.
That my very existence I owe to you
I'm ever so grateful for that.
Fees paid on first of every month
money sent for boarding, lodging, books and
miscellany.

Never ever felt want of any kind.
Ever so grateful I am
for your every little act.
Only during vacation you wished me to stay
back and study hard
I must become a big barrister, doctor
or professor—whatever it was,
it had to be big.
That was your only little wish.

When middle of semester
was called by your neighbours

you were already gone far away
holding on to your breath just enough
to look at your son
after a decade and a half
to see how 'big' he had become.

But I didn't want to become so 'big'
that the tiny room where you lived
where real 'big' people came
I was told,
in the darkness of the night
would suffocate me.
I'm still grateful to you
for every act of yours.
Will I ever be able to
pay my dues?

Love abandoned

You were in a tearing hurry
galloping away
marking new milestones
on the way.
I tried keeping pace
but the finishing line
went farther and farther away.
The gap between us
got wider and wider.
I tried warning you
against racing this race
The thirst would be unquenchable
I said—
The greed insatiable.

You let Love fall
by the wayside
covered in dust
after you raced past.
Love—nurtured by the two of us
not so long ago.

My heart broke
to see it abandoned,
orphaned, unrecognisable
in the dusty racing track.

Them and me

Meandering narrow lanes
flanked by shops on both sides
selling wares of all kinds...
from tiny Shiva-lingas, temple accessories
to battery-operated toy steamers
in red and blue
going round and round
sputtering water
in a water-filled small container.

Small shops selling sarees and thin shawls;
rows of tiny outlets outside the tiny shops
selling colourful glass bangles,
bindis and sindoor,
jhumkas and nose-rings.
Beneath their bamboo tables
narrow open drains flowing with water
coming out of the several small temples
surrounding the famous
Vishwanath temple.

The gulli always muddy
with water sometimes spilling over
from the drain.
And in the rainy season
puddles forming everywhere.
Long queues already forming
since five in the morning,
greeted me when freshly bathed
in the five-star hotel
I arrived to have darshan.
My sandals placed over the pile of
chappals and shoes of devotees
in niches and corners
beside the several shop doors.
A little uncertainly and a tad consciously
I too joined the queue.

Suddenly from nowhere
stout men appeared—
head clean-shaven
wearing white dhoti kurta

with ochre-coloured scarf
thrown across their shoulders
asking me to come out
of the serpentine queue
and have a special darshan too.

Why me? Thought I.
Is it writ large on my face
that I don't belong here?
That I have not travelled from
Madurai, Kanyakumari,
24-Parganas or Alwar,
but from the capital of the country?
That I do not belong to this class of pilgrims
who can brave the heat, the dust, the crowd?

Breaking hesitantly away from the queue
telling myself, had I not felt claustrophobic
I too would have stood
like them in the queue.
I went with one of the pandas

and reached the Sanctum Sanctorum
in no time.

Coming out of the Exit gate
into another by-lane,
was greeted with the sight of
some score of widows
clad in sarees not so white—
head covered, eyes blank
on both sides of the lane,
sitting with aluminium bowls—
twisted, discoloured
with a couple of coins in them
looking at me with supplication.

Bengali widows mostly
left at Benaras station stealthily—
their off-spring promising to return soon.
Were those promises meant to be kept?
That is, well but anyone's guess.

Soon the children would be going back

with hearts that are guilt-free.
Kashi is the place to die in—
their birth-givers going surely to heaven,
freed from the ceaseless cycle of birth and death.

Leaving ten-rupee notes in each bowl
I slowly walk to the waiting car,
not devoid of embarrassment and shame
at the commonality between
these widows' off-springs and me,

the disparity between the devotees
standing equanimously in the queue;
the widows sitting patiently
with begging bowls
and me.

Narrow strip of sky

That narrow strip of sky you see
between the two sky-scrapers,
if you look at it long and hard
you might catch a glimpse of
a kite—
not a plethora of colourful kites
vying with each other
for supremacy.

Or if you are lucky
you might also see
the arc of the moon—
No, not the whole galaxy

that you and I
would hazard a guess
as to which star
is your little sister
and which my mother.

Those were days of plenty—
of expansivenes.

Days didn't end
with the setting of the sun
nor the nights arrive
with the lit- up street lights.
Mother's half a dozen calls
would see us reluctantly
trudge towards home.
When indoor games and outdoor
kept us on our toes.
Story books, exchanged with friends,
finished before home-work began.
Ghost stories lapped up
while clinging to grandpa
and tales of Princes and princesses
that ended with
'they lived happily ever after.'

When our laughter echoed
in our neighbours' houses
and friends barged into
our call-bell-free houses.

Everything seems to have shrunk now
shrivelled like my mother's
puckered hands
—hearts, houses, minds.
Too small to hold
those large extended families
and each child's wild fantasies.

Can that history repeat itself?
Well, that story is for another day.

Dreams cheat

Parched land
as far as the eyes can see—
fissures as deep as the furrows
on the forehead of the man
sitting haunched up,
shading with his wrinkled hand
the woe-begone eyes
with powered glasses
from the merciless June sun.

The relentless summer heat
with not a drop of rain;
the dried-up river-beds and wells
have sounded the death-knell.

His wife sitting in front
of the thatched hut
with their baby at her breast
trying to suckle
from her almost-dried breast.

With a jutting forehead

and sparse brown hair,
the pot-bellied, mal-nourished
rickety baby
raises his large eyes
from his mother's breast
seeming to empathise
with her pain—
deluded as he has been
yet again.
He dozes off
in fitful sleep
and dreams such
glorious Dreams.

Dreams have a large heart
unlike many.
They keep giving you
till you go crazy.
Gallons of milk
in mother's breast—
two square meals

on your parents' plate.
A field rich in harvest,
a flowing river,
a heavy downpour
washing away yesterday's
uncertainties and tears
from mother's face;
reviving the jasmine creeper
on their hut's naked roof
making his mother
string again
a garland everyday
to adorn her long, lush hair.

But Dreams have a funny way
of suddenly coming to an end.
Making him stare again
at yesterday's bleakness
rolling over
to today
and tomorrow.

The confluence

Another batch of freshers
with eager expectant faces
greeted me with breathless
anticipation
their bright 'good morning'
wishes.

Along with their uniforms
they seem to have shed their inhibitions—
these girls—turned out in
smart, trendy dresses.
As if each one trying to make
a style statement—
each one just stepping out
of a parlour.
With painted nails and lips
and branded accessories.

Suddenly my eyes fell
on a group of
six or seven girls

occupying a less conspicuous
space,
looking at me with the same
eagerness.
And yet there was a faint hint
of doubt and fear.
Have they made a mistake
leaving their all-familiar
places?
I smiled at them.
My eyes assuring them
that the distance they have
traversed
is no mean achievement.
There are many more
milestones
to cross.
They are not children
of a lesser God.

They smiled back.
And I began my lecture.

Childhood reclaimed

Footloose and fancy-free in a foreign land
hopping from one cobbled stone
to another
watched by the silvery Moon above
indulgently.

The Moon smiles at the gay abandon
of this earthy creature
who has found spring in her steps
taking fistful of pleasure
child-like— in the vast open spaces

collecting oyster shells on the beaches
plucking apples from the stooping branches
getting drenched in the first
monsoon showers
playing hide-and-seek with children
in the park.

She reclaims her childhood
left behind—
lost somewhere
trampled upon
by adult responsibilities.

The burning hall

Engrossed they were in the war scenes
unfolding on the large screen.
The magic aura produced by the heroes
had the capacity crowd totally spellbound.

More so because it was a theme
dear to their hearts—
the glory and laurels
brought by the martyrs.

Suddenly from nowhere
the smoke billowed.
An ear-splitting noise
that seemed to vibrate through the hall.

Helter - skelter they ran
in pitch darkness.
Not knowing what had struck them
with such harshness.

Mothers screaming for their children,
the old and the young dashing for the 'Exit,'

which somebody had, for some odd reason,
locked from outside.

Some fell on the floor
asphyxiated.
Others ran over them in a last
ditch-effort to run to safety.

Meanwhile, more smoke
black and angry,
entered the hall
from every little opening.

Hot like an oven
the auditorium had become,
so they ran to the toilet
to wet their scalding bodies.

And there they were found,
lying unconscious.
Both the rich and the poor.
As Death makes no distinction.

Chappals and purses,
li'l shoes and glasses,
remain mute witnesses
to the grim tragedy just unfolded.

Bodies draped in
shrouds white
lined the corridors of hospital
that Friday night.
Mothers clinging to their young ones
even in death,
perished as they had
in one swift breath.

Why did it happen?
How did it happen?
Well, enquiries as usual
have been ordered
to fix responsibility
and to find out
who bribed whom.

Meanwhile, the survivors were left
To carry their dead—
the victims of another
man-made tragedy
from the fiery grave
to the burning ghats
For the last rites.

The vacant space

The place you vacated on my bed
the other day
still lies vacant.
The warmth on your side of the bed
has turned icy cold.
My deep breathing cannot catch
your favourite fragrance.
My arm stretches in vain
to put across your breasts.
A few strands of hair on your pillow
I wind round my finger,
trying to smell
the special scent of your hair.

A lot has changed.
But the moon's the same
and is again peeping through
the broken window pane,
disappointed to see
the empty space
on the bed;

had hoped to see
two people in wakeful nights
talking and making love.
She is my comrade, my soul mate
who understands completely
the pain of desertion.

My father

A bundle of energy
at an age when most men
lead a sedate life
dependent on others.

Thin, bent a little with age,
he would spring up
when any of us needed him
when in dire straights.

Had no degree in painting, pottery
or music. But the qualities were
essentially intrinsic.
A pity none of us has father's
pearl-like hand-writing—
but we were blessed to sleep
some glorious sleep
to his soulful lullabies.

A man smart with household gadgets,
he had a penchant for opening up
transistors and wrist-watches.

It invited, no doubt,
our mother's wrath
but he would re-assemble
the precision parts
with a panache.

But when he tried doing the same
with our black-and-white T.V set
he was obviously upset
with the resistance he met
and a warning not to fiddle with
electronic gadgets.
Such was our father that he
renounced his own interests
to the point of
self-abnegation.

Never complained of uneasiness
or pain, when dengue's
first red patches
surfaced on his body.

All our lives we had only

taken from him
given very little.

When paralysis struck his body
partially,
due to heavy smoking
since college days,
a large patch in his
chest x-ray
sealed his fate.

He still had the desire to live.
I had seen it in his eyes
when he looked at me
from his hospital bed.

But having a will,
is not good enough
however much
the doctors may say.
The gods and my father's children
failed him that day.

Parallel lines

Walking down two parallel lines
you and I talking of this and that
mundane things—all inconsequential
better left unsaid.
They showed the labour on your part
the effort on mine.

Did I hear you say those magic words?
No—they are the sighs under your breath.
Did you hold out your hand
to hold mine?
No—your hand is firmly in the pocket
of your jacket.
Did I feel you ruffle my hair
in that good old endearing way?
It is the breeze this time
making a fool of me;
watching me imagining
the rakish familiar smile
at the corner of your lips
causing my pulse to race once,

my heart to skip a beat.

Wish we were walking a single lane
and not two parallel railway tracks.
From the window of a train
I have seen them umpteen times—
the lines coming near
touching each other
before zigzagging away—
keeping the decorum of a distance.

Let us touch each other,
feel,
hold on tight
our entwined fingers.
No need to keep
the decorum of a distance.
We are not tracks—
but were lovers once.

My shame

'One more leave
And you are out—' I warned.
'Tired I am of your excuses
your problems, your never-ending woes.'

The incessant rains
of the last one week
have penetrated through
her thatched roof—she said,
and spoilt the grains, the clothes,
her children's school bags
and everything else.

Why did she not come yesterday then?
I thundered. Did the sun not come out
for sometime?
With downcast eyes and in a voice
no more than a whisper, she said—

It was spent guarding the notes
laid out to dry in the sunlight—
her whole month's salary of
five thousand and five fifty rupees.

The image is all too vivid for me.
That rectangular slice of sunlight
that falls in front of her home
is sole witness to her story
of want and deprivation—
neglect and privation.

It is time for rumination for me
—some soul-searching and deep
mortification.
The Sumatis of the world,
 whose appearance at the doorstep every
morning

like a breath of fresh air,
like a cool breeze in a summer's night,
like a drop of water in a parched throat,
will never learn to complain
against anybody
—man or God—

But will pick up the pieces of their lives
again tomorrow,
once the vagaries of the weather
are over for today.

A truth

Difficult to describe the place.
Something that doesn't seem to gell
with the reality outside—
cars zooming past
horns of trucks and buses
the milling crowd rushing,
racing to reach some place in life.

None takes time out to turn
their head—
have a look at the place—
a grey building
surrounded by tall banyan trees
crows cawing in the branches
can't diminish the solemnity
of the place.
And river Yamuna flowing
serenely by.
It is not important in their
scheme of things today.
Will think about it when
the actual time comes.

Did Time come for this young man?
Did he come announcing his
impending arrival?
Commanding him to get ready?
But today we have come
to bid him a final farewell.

Laid on the cemented platform
with sandalwood paste smeared
(Did I see a serene, benign,
all-knowing smile on his face?
an oblique hint
That this is as real as life itself?)

As his father, bent-double
with the weight of the reality
performed the last rites
amidst chanting of Gayatri mantra

I was face -to -face
with Life's greatest truth—
Death is not
negation of Life.

The rising and setting sun

The bright red 'bindi' on her forehead,
like the big red ball in the eastern sky,
was put along with 'sindoor' in the
parting of her hair,
amidst lot of laughter and 'uludhwani,'
blowing of conch shell and clapping.

Someone covered her head with a red
'Lajjawastra'—reminding her of a
woman's ornament—her modesty
which she would do well to adorn
in her groom's house.

Like the morning sun
her arrival will usher in
prosperity.
The red 'bindi,'—the marker of her
husband's well-being,
and the red and white bangles,
—symbols of her new status
all of which, she was told

will have to be upheld.

Is this the same sun,
red and orange,
but all splashed across a vast space?
Yes, it happens when the setting sun
takes with it all hopes
one pins on a new bride.
The red 'bindi' erased in a hurry
spreads across her forehead—
The bangles, red and white
and the red sari have to be quickly taken off,
her modesty is in white now—
marker of purity.

The white Moon has come up.
Is there a black mark on her?
'I told you right in the beginning
The girl was not right for our sonny.'

sindoor: a marker of a woman's married state—
red vermillion.

uludhwani: sound produced by the tongue by
married women during any auspicious ceremony.

conch: a palm-sized white shell which produces
sound when air blown into it.—blown during
auspicious ceremonies.

Lajjawastra: sari put on a Bengali bride's head
signifying her modesty when her husband puts
red vermillion in the parting of her hair at the
marriage ceremony.

My Valentine's Day

I went out to dinner myself
dressed in the yellow sari
I had gifted myself.
Picked up a red rose on
the way
and tucked it in the bun
at the nape of the neck.

The place was unusually
crowded
and why should it not be
it was Valentine's Day—
The day of love and
friendship.

As I moved through the tables
occupied by young couples
to reach my favourite corner,
quite a few heads turned
to look at the woman
with streaks of white
in her hair

and a red rose
tucked in there.

A dash of red lipstick
and danglers in her ears.
And when she ordered
a glass of red wine
a few chuckles and sneers
from neighbouring tables
could not, however, diminish
the heady feeling
the memories brought
as they rushed in
of such Valentine's days
spent together
in this very corner place.

What is today celebrated as
Valentine's day
is our Wedding Anniversary.
He many not be with me
physically

but resides in my
every breath.

The last five years
I have been coming here
alone
taking in my stride
the side- long glances
and twitching of lips
of young couples.

I can imagine what is
going on
in their minds.
An old woman—
pushing seventy
making a pathetic attempt
to celebrate alone
the day of lovers
with wine and flowers.

Now it is my turn to return

the smug smile.
Their declaration
of undying love
for each other
will, in most cases
end up in a hotel room
or a cheap one-room set—
all physical—all carnal
which, alas, may not see
the blooming of flowers
of the next spring.

While I proudly carry on
the torch of our eternal love
whose flame will continue
to burn
as long as I live.
It has seen
forty years of joy
—not unalloyed though,
fights, arguments, tiffs

happened,
but they were storms
that blew away.
Not tornadoes
that ever threatened
to usurp
the place of pure love.

It was my way of
commemorating
our journey of togetherness,
exactly the way
he would have
loved to see me
spend the day.

It was not a neat drink.
That glass of red wine
was a cocktail of
love, zest, romance
and memory.

Embrace life

In this barren human land
not a tree in sight
to give the much-needed shade
or in whose dense foliage
I could lose myself —
hide from curious glare
my ignominy and shame.

That one mistake,
will I be branded for life?
Why live at all
if in this whole wide world
can't find a soul
who will not judge me,
crucify me, every single day?

Suddenly heard
as if temple bells—

Don't be so harsh on yourself.
Look at the radiant sky, and
the rainbow in all its hues.

The sharp wind
cannot dislodge
the tiny cuckoo
from the tree-top
nor the mother squirrel
from reaching her babes.

Open your heart.
Christ is knocking
at the door.
This is the day of mercy.
Go out.
Embrace life.

Sign of our times

It is the sign of our times, dear
It is the sign of our times.
People boast of pockets deep.
Are feted for their rhetorical speech.
Termed cultured and elite
judging by the English
they speak with a flourish.

Politically correct answers,
measured words, plastic smiles—
indifference, impatience
marking their restless profiles.

Tolerance—a thing of the past.
Acceptance—an alien word.
Jumping the queue anywhere, routine.
A young man lying bleeding
on the road—
by an errant minor driver mowed,
is with utter callousness videoed.

Me, mine, myself

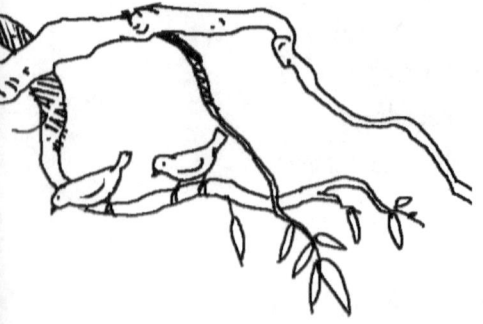

the only reflexive pronouns
in one's vocabulary.
Consumerism—the buzzword.
The Law of diminishing marginal utility
turned on its head.

Where are we heading?
A vast abyss, a bottomless pit?

Birth of a song

The haunting melody
still echoing among the hills,
the vibrant valley
and the flowing fjords,
on the shepherd's flute
the maiden's lips;
took birth from the poet's pen
on one of those moonless nights
dark and sombre
with only the beloved's memory
for company.

Born a woman

If to breathe is to live,
I am alive.
If to be born a homosapien
the best possible birth on earth,
then I am the coveted species.
If to be born a woman,
to be blessed the most,
then I am blessed indeed.
Because I am God's 'finest creation.'

Or am I indeed?
Do you use me as a pawn
in your game of chess
because I am the finest?
Make me go through
Tests of fire
Because I burn easily?
Buy and sell me—
Your Lakshmi, Saraswati Parvati?

Today on Durga puja

you will worship me.
I want neither the pedestal
nor the doormat.
But simply the satisfaction
of a life
lived on my terms.

Billoo

He is, to everyone
The dim-witted Billoo.
Tall, lanky—a little light
in the head.
To all their query, he smiles
his adorable smile.
And when he stutters
to make a point,
the snigger all around
makes it worse still.
Anybody is free to make
a dig at him
It is everyone's prerogative
it seems.

The twelve -year old flunked
in the same class twice.
Plays with children
half his age. Feels safe,
loved in their company.

Watching boys, his own age,
playing cricket,
Billoo came there unobtrusively.
And as the ball came his way suddenly
he caught it instinctively.
The roar of laughter and
shouts of 'Dravid, our own Jonty Rhodes'
filling the air
sent a sense of embarrassment
 through his body
 —names unfamiliar, strange.
But the fun, he knew, was at his expense.
He smiled that silly smile again
But it failed to reach up to his eyes,
this time.

Someone shouted 'enough Billoo.
Now go back to where you belong—
to play hopscotch jump.'
As he turned slowly back
the derisory laughter of the boys
followed Billoo all through.

The last afternoon

Reading from the Rubaiyat,
you and I
spent that autumn afternoon—
the languid placid afternoon
with dry leaves flying around,
oblivious of the constant clattering
of the sparrows—
or the pair of squirrels
stopping in their run
to gaze at us.

Your black hair
like the dense clouds
gathering in the eastern sky,
started to fly
all over my face,
the scent of roses
wafting in my nostrils.
And when you started humming
Tagore's Bipul Taranga Re
in Raag Bhimpalasi

I was transported
to a heavenly plane.

Did you also feel
the current of unlimited joy
in the poet's song
as I did?
Nothing short of elixir
was it for me
whose memory would
see me through.
And you?
Did you also wish
the partly-covered sun
would not set?
That the birds would not so soon
start to return to their nest?

But Nature does not stop in its track
If only one of the lovers
wants it to.

You had to return
as you did
to begin your future
the next day
that promised of more joy
than our past and present
spent together.

My immunity strengthened
by the magical potion
of the elixir
braced up my shattered,
tattered inside
enough for me
to bring up an apology of a smile

when

in that seemingly
melodious afternoon
someone somewhere
sang a note out of tune.

The theft

Yes, she stole it.
How come no one in the house
got to know of it?
When did she do it?

In between cooking and packing tiffins
washing and ironing
cleaning and sleeping?

How dare she filch it?
It should have been used
to do some more house-work.

Cleaning should have been done twice.
More cobwebs could surely have been
found somewhere and removed.
More clothes and bed-sheets ironed.

No special dishes made for days
No delicacies one has tasted
on any of the holidays.

Sheer negligence.

Not to be condoned.
She purloined it
to knit and stitch
sketch and do batik paint?
read story books and write too?
The housewife has stolen time,
indulged herself,
opened the window of her room
to let the wind carry
her songs of spring
to far-away lands
to fields and meadows
and mingle them with those
of other women
who have dared to open
their windows.

The leaf-hopper

Perched on the green banana leaf
subsuming herself
completely camouflaged
making no attempt to stand out
though her colour is no less green
texture no less bright.

In fact, her texture
has a mosaic of patterns
denied to the plain banana leaf.
She can fly,
can hop;
while the plant is so static.
Yet, she is resigned
playing second-fiddle.

Those who can spot her
gaze at her
and not the leaf.
That is satisfaction enough
for the leaf-hopper.
And with her surrounding
the more she blends in.

Autumnal leaves

Sitting by my hospital bed
holding my hand
with prayers on your lips,
pleading with me to open my eyes,
you, my son, please don't
make things tough for me.

I have already made
a truce with God, dear.
The bright light is
beckoning me.
Don't pull me the other way.
Between life and death
there is that thin thread
loosen the kite reel, son.
Let go off me.
I can almost sense freedom
flying amongst the clouds.

Those spoons of water
you are pouring in my mouth
is Gangajal for me.

Don't err thinking
it is Ambrosia.
Grieve not son.
Nature does not like a vacuum.
If the brown autumnal leaves fall
So do tender green leaves sprout.

One death does not mean the end.
A new-born's first cry somewhere
will usher in a new dawn.

The flag

A whole city as if under siege.
The sporadic incidents of breaking
of barricades
and provoking the police
have suddenly and shockingly taken on
the proportion of a war.
A rabid mob
burning, looting, threatening—
brandishing arms
carrying different coloured flags
establishing their different identities
of caste, creed, sub-caste, religion,
state, language—you name it.

From the vantage point of my terrace
the significance of the flags
gets diluted
and who is fighting for which flag
is drowned in the mad din of
individual stake-holders,
erased by the blackness

of the night.

What stands out in the darkest
of the dark night
is the tri-colour flying in all its glory
atop the India Gate.
The one flag for whose honour
our brave sons in khaki
are fighting and dying smiling.
And when they come back
in coffins
it's the same flag that so proudly
carries them in its arms.

The scenes presented pictures
in contrast.
And gave me enough food for thought
in another black night
when sleep eluded me.

Then and now

Rains splashing across
a vast expanse
Nature's fury as far as
the eyes can see.
Two palm tress got uprooted
a few tin sheds of neighbouring houses
blew away.
But for her and her two friends
It was time for fun and freedom.

All of ten years of age—Usha, Maloti
and Beena
tucked their saris up,
waited for the rains
to subside a little
and ran to the banks of the pond
to float their paper boats
and long banana leaves.

But that was—then.
That was—there.

Here, through the barbed window panes
Usha can see only the rooftops
of a few houses.
And crows shaking their rain-drenched bodies
cawing in, oh, such raucous voices.
But for Usha now, their call is
like the chime of temple bells—
like the sweet chant of
Kirtan and Pala.
A clarion call for freedom?
Something wet her cheeks
(Not the rains surely?)
In this match-box of a room—
her room of two years
something blurred her vision
and obliterated from her consciousness
her past.

And a voice—
(The crow's voice? So harsh this time?)
No, it is the Chimera's

bringing her back to the present
reminding her it's time
to earn her keep.
Customers are Gods after all
To be worshipped.

No, she did not think
even for once
she would be worshipped
as of yore
on the day of Ashtami.

Lying buried

You've aged before your time.
Those curly crop of hair
over a fair round face
aquired silver streaks prematurely;
the broad forehead
developed deep grooves
narrating several untold tales;
the hands—flour-white—are coarse,
rough from house-hold chores—
showing mountain-top of prominent veins
that you can't slip on
those two gold bangles kept in your cupboard
for occasions like Puja or a family wedding.

How much pain will you
continue to bury?
they are piling up
only to explode one day.
Break free mother
or I will exhume them;
count each one of them
that you have so painstakingly hidden
from even their perpetrators.

Lesson learnt

A tad pensive
sitting by the train window
mulling over what Life has denied me
what could have been,
should have been mine,
snatched by powers greater than me.

Suddenly saw pretty flowers in clusters
on both sides of the track
moving their heads
as if in unison
with a little whiff of the breeze.
All of them—the pansy, the African violet,
and the iris
seemed to be saying to me

get up and dance with me,
this is not the time to ponder,
or be angry.
Lift your spirits up
and dance with me.

The rains lash us.
The hailstorm does
all it can to damage us.
But the first ray of the Sun
after the storm and the rain
tells us to ope our eyes
and get back to doing
what we are good at—
moving and dancing
with the gentle breeze.

Change what you can.
Let go what you can't.

The morning after

There is a yearning for coupling
in the meeting of the rain and the river
Love's boundaries broken.
There was some resistance initially
but when the clouds had given their all
how long could the coy banks hold?—
sensed immense pleasure
in total surrender, the violation.

After the torrential rain,
when the night gave cover
to their union,
the morning sun saw a new river
bathed fresh after the night-long adventure.
Its banks freshly drawn,
assuming a new identity
like a bride looking radiant
the morning after
the consummation.

The pebbles

The pebbles on the shore
shining white, pink or grey
some with light blue veins in them—
different in size and shape
big and small, round, spherical
standing out in their own
characteristic way.

Came the tempestuous tide
lashing against the shore.
Some got picked up
and whipped back again.
A few cowered,
made peace with the waves
and went along with them.

Some held their ground and
are a proud rocky conglomerate
amidst the far-receding
tide and the sky.

The dawn must come

The blackness of the night
suits you today.
Putting the key in the lock-hole
does not need any dexterity
you have been doing it
even in the darkness of the
lunar eclipse—
entering the house, feeling your way
through the bedroom, kitchen,
and bathroom
on those nights of load-shedding—
ghost stories never bothered you.

Tonight you seem to be fumbling—
lighting the candle reluctantly.
The familiar shadow of the
mango tree in the courtyard
assuming a sinister meaning.
Bats flapping wings in the lonely night—
you used to laughingly say
are welcoming you.

It is not welcome tonight.
Clanking of vessels in the kitchen
startles you today
when every tiny jar there
you know, like the back
of your hand.
Why wary of your own footsteps?
Your own slanting shadow
on the staircase?
Your own dim reflection in the mirror?
Why shudder seeing patterns
formed on the floor
by the flickering candle
in the breeze?
It is normal, routine.

The blackness of the night
suits you today. In fact,
you desire it.

Clothes a little dishevelled,
hair normally wieldy,
looking like a storm has
blown through them.

The large black eyes,
in whose depth
the whole world could drown,
are hesitating to meet their reflection
in the mirror.

Don't wish for the night to continue.
With the first ray of the sun
must your bugle sound.

Identity

Same time, same channel
same people on the panel
questions more or less the same
asked by viewers of them.

Problems in marriage,
lovers' tiff, broken promises—
all's the same.
What is it then
that has drawn her to the T.V set
all these days?

It is the request
the viewers make
to the counsellors
not to take their names
in case someone known to them
should happen to identify them.

What irony, what a quirk of fate
she thought—
she had the urge

to dial the number
splashed across the screen
and ask them, why the shame?
When they have an identity
to be proud of
where's the cause for disgrace?
While she, Anamika—the nameless
denied a father's name,
her mother asked
not to give her birth.
'It was a youthful aberration,'
he had said.
His whole life lay in front,
his reputation would be at stake.

Thanks to her mother's grit
she saw the light of day.
But a father's name
she will never have.
Nor would she be
ashamed of that.

I know why

You didn't want to cry
when the world was rejoicing
on the birth of a new millennium.
Your individual grief must not mar
the collective euphoria—
celebrations that will continue for
months together.

I know why
you are getting
drenched in the rain.

The continuous flow of tears
like a tap left running
will go unnoticed.
Emotions, bottled up
for far too long
can get frozen
like taps in winter.
You needed a spur
to melt it all down—

the running water will
save the pipe from bursting.

Today, exactly after a month,
the picture of your still-born child
is coming too vividly to mind.
I know why
you are getting drenched
in the rain.

Let the waters wash away
all your pent-up sorrow.
Nine months of wait
is no less
than the wait
for a millennium—
the hopes, the dreams.
The morning was pregnant
with new possibilities.

On the first day

of the new millennium,
you wanted to look
in the eyes of your angel.
She could well be
the millennium's child.

I know why
you are getting drenched
in the rain
you don't wish to sound
a discordant note
when the world is listening
to the music of the spheres.

That's me

Shout, holler, scream.
Do something.
Abuses—the vituperative outbursts
I can take, and your acerbic barbs.
Absorb your splenetic caustic remarks
which once used to hit me
like projectiles.

It was always one-sided
like shadow -boxing.
I was your favourite
punching bag.

So, don't lie there so quiet.
The eerie stillness of the room
is gnawing at me
mocking me almost.

Nurse I will, don't you fear.
Say atleast one last time
you wronged me.

Don't look at me like that.
Want to make amends?
bridge the distance?
Are those beseeching eyes
begging for forgiveness?
Forgiven I have, dear.
Commiserations come naturally to me—don't
wish to carry the baggage
to my next life.

But forget I can't.
And I will not.
Never liked a one-sided fight.
Not then.
Not now.

Hope

I saw the waterfalls
in her exultation
the fast-flowing river
in her banter,
clouds almost touching ground
when she stood up
with her hair cascading down;
and the dark stillness of the night
in her large limpid eyes.

I also saw a vision of Kali
And Mahisasurmardini
spewing fire from her eyes
in her challenge
to take on the world,
brushing aside with one stroke
of her hand
all the garbage piled up
on her way
and picking up with the other,
young girls waiting

by the wayside
looking up to her
for deliverance.
I go home smiling.
My faith reinforced
once again
by her acts of courage.

Oxygen for life

Moving her own wheel chair
with her wrinkled hands
the frail old lady
passed me by
as I was sipping coffee
at Cafe Coffee Day.

And when I boarded the bus
to look round the city
she was there in the queue
before me.
I took my seat beside her
and struck up a conversation
to get to know her.

She was going to the museum
(like me,) she said
and then have lunch
at some warm cosy place,
buy her provisions for the week
on the way back home

and rustle up a light dinner
before retiring to bed.

This has been her routine
every single day—
to visit either the park or the opera,
the theatre or simply
the river bank across the street.

And take in the scene around,
the warmth of the people she met
the laughter and sunshine
the hustle -bustle of the promenade
and come back home
with oxygen
to live another day.

A kaleidoscope

It was a kaleidoscope.
It belonged to the realm of dreams.
I felt inspired—
wanted to write a poem
drawing my theme
from the fleet of boats and steamers
rowing on the Rhine river—
the mountains dotted with ski resorts,
Lake Lucerne,
summit Jungfrau on the Alps—
green villages with pretty houses
picture -perfect.

Sitting on the banks of bluish green water
of Limmat river,
watching grizzled clouds
kissing the majestic mountains
on the distant horizon

they beckoning me—
making me breathe in

lungs - full of oxygen—
inviting me to sail
to a Paradisal
ethereal zone,

I could not but
respond to their call;
and as I went
farther and farther
away from the bank
there was no looking back.

A job to do

The wood continues to burn.
Now and then red embers fly.
Smoke making the scene hazy,
burning the eyes of the mourners.
Or are they the tears
that refuse to die down?

But the wood can't afford
to smart over the deaths.
It is born to burn
one body after the other.
Peace is in acceptance.
It cools the throbbing pain.

When water is sprinkled
over the dying smouldering flame
some sparks still fly—
they have to.
Some bones stubbornly hold on
to their physical entity.
Detaching them completely

finally, irrevocably,
requires endless patience,
years of dedication.

The logs have a job to do.
It's not true
that they don't wish to shed
a tear or two.

About the Author

Born and brought up in Delhi, Shanta Dutta Roy did her masters in English Literature from Delhi University and Ph.d from Banaras Hindu University.

She has been associated with teaching literature and language to students of Maitreyi College, Delhi University for more than four decades.

Her field of specialisation is modern British poetry specially Philip Larkin's work. Apart from her interest in English, she is equally fascinated by Bengali literature. She is passionate about writing English poetry, and keen about music—both Indian classical and Rabindra Sangeet. She loves to travel around the world.

She has two sons residing in Dubai and Canada with their families. Her husband Bikash is a metallurgical engineer by profession.

www.ingramcontent.com/pod-product-compliance
Lightning Source LLC
Chambersburg PA
CBHW030312130626
46549CB00002B/818

9789388247481